CYBERSECURITY

FROM BASICS TO EXPERT

VIPUL BAIBHAV

Made with ♥ on the Notion Press Platform
www.notionpress.com

To all those working to keep our digital world safe and secure, we dedicate this book. Your dedication and expertise are invaluable in the fight against cyber threats, and we hope that this book serves as a helpful resource in your journey to become experts in cybersecurity.

I dedicate this book to

- My family or loved ones, for their support and encouragement as you pursued your studies in cybersecurity
- My colleagues or mentors in the field of Cybersecurity, who have inspired me and guided you in my career
- Students or trainees, as a way of sharing your knowledge and experience with the next generation of cybersecurity professionals.
- And all my readers who wants to pursue their career in the field of cyber security.

Contents

Foreword

"As the digital landscape continues to evolve, so too does the need for strong cybersecurity measures. In this age of interconnected devices and networks, it is more important than ever to prioritize the protection of our personal and professional data from cyber threats.

"In "Cybersecurity: From Basics to Experts," readers will find a comprehensive guide to understanding and implementing effective cybersecurity practices. From the basics of strong password creation and two-factor authentication, to more advanced concepts such as cloud security and incident response, this book covers a wide range of topics that are essential for anyone looking to improve their cybersecurity posture.

"Whether you are new to the field or an experienced professional, "Cybersecurity: From Basics to Experts" has something to offer. I highly recommend this book to anyone looking to build their knowledge and expertise in cybersecurity, and I am confident that it will serve as a valuable resource for years to come."

Preface

"As the author of "Cybersecurity: From Basics to Experts," we are proud to present this comprehensive guide to understanding and implementing effective cybersecurity measures. In today's digital age, the protection of computer systems, networks, and devices from cyber threats is of utmost importance for individuals and organizations alike.

"In this book, I have covered a range of topics that are essential for anyone looking to improve their cybersecurity posture. From the basics of strong password creation and two-factor authentication, to more advanced concepts such as cloud security and incident response, we aim to provide a complete overview of the field.

"I have written this book with the goal of making cybersecurity accessible and understandable to readers of all levels of experience. Whether you are just starting out in the field or are an experienced professional, we hope that you will find valuable insights and practical tips within these pages.

"I am grateful for the opportunity to share my knowledge and expertise with you, and we hope that "Cybersecurity: From Basics to Experts" will serve as a valuable resource for anyone looking to build their skills in this vital field."

Acknowledgements

"I would like to express our heartfelt gratitude to all those who have contributed to the creation of "Cybersecurity: From Basics to Experts."

"First and foremost, I would like to thank our families and loved ones for their unwavering support and encouragement throughout the writing process. Your patience and understanding have meant the world to us.

"I am also grateful to our colleagues and mentors in the field of cybersecurity, who have generously shared their knowledge and experience with us. Your guidance and insights have been invaluable in the development of this book.

"I would also like to thank the editorial and production teams at Notion Press for their hard work and dedication in bringing this book to fruition. Your professionalism and expertise have been greatly appreciated.

"Finally, we would like to thank our readers for choosing "Cybersecurity: From Basics to Experts." We hope that this book serves as a valuable resource in your journey to become experts in cybersecurity.

"Thank you all for your support and contributions. I could not have done this without you."

Prologue

As we enter the digital age, the importance of cybersecurity cannot be overstated. Every day, our personal and professional lives are increasingly reliant on computer systems, networks, and devices, and the protection of this digital infrastructure is essential.

"Unfortunately, with the growth of the internet and the proliferation of connected devices, the risk of cyber threats has also increased. From data breaches and malware attacks, to phishing scams and ransomware, the threats facing our digital world are numerous and varied.

In response to this growing threat, the field of cybersecurity has emerged as a vital and rapidly-evolving discipline. Professionals in this field are dedicated to the protection of computer systems, networks, and devices from digital attacks, theft, and damage.

In "Cybersecurity: From Basics to Experts," we aim to provide a comprehensive guide to understanding and implementing effective cybersecurity measures. From the basics of strong password creation and two-factor authentication, to more advanced concepts such as cloud security and incident response, we cover a wide range of topics that are essential for anyone looking to improve their cybersecurity posture.

Whether you are new to the field or an experienced professional, we hope that this book serves as a valuable resource in your journey to become an expert in cybersecurity. The threats facing our digital world are real, but with the right knowledge and tools, we can stay safe and secure online.

CHAPTER ONE

Introduction to Cybersecurity

Cybersecurity is the practice of protecting computer systems, networks, and devices from digital attacks, theft, and damage. It is a rapidly-evolving field that is essential for individuals and organizations to prioritize in order to prevent data breaches, unauthorized access, and other cyber threats.

The history of cybersecurity dates back to the 1960s, when the first computer viruses were created. As the internet and computer technology have grown and become more widespread, the need for effective cybersecurity measures has also increased. Today, cybersecurity professionals work to protect a wide range of systems, including personal computers, servers, mobile devices, and even critical infrastructure such as power plants and transportation systems.

There are many different aspects to cybersecurity, including network security, cloud security, mobile security, and risk management. Professionals in the field may specialize in one or more of these areas, and may also be responsible for compliance with relevant laws and regulations.

As the digital landscape continues to evolve, so too does the field of cybersecurity. New technologies, such as the internet of things (IoT) and artificial intelligence (AI), bring with them new security challenges and opportunities. It is important for cybersecurity professionals to stay up-to-date on the latest developments and best practices in order to effectively protect against cyber threats.

CHAPTER TWO

Basic Cybersecurity Measures

There are several basic measures that individuals and organizations can take to improve their cybersecurity posture and protect against cyber threats. These measures include:

- Use strong and unique passwords: Use a combination of letters, numbers, and special characters in your passwords, and avoid using the same password for multiple accounts.
- Enable two-factor authentication: Two-factor authentication (2FA) adds an extra layer of security by requiring you to provide a second form of verification, such as a code sent to your phone, in addition to your password.
- Keep your software and devices up to date: Regularly update your operating system, web browsers, and other software to protect against security vulnerabilities that may have been discovered.
- Be cautious when clicking links or downloading attachments: Be wary of links or attachments in emails or messages from unknown sources, as they may contain malware.
- Use a firewall: A firewall is a security system that monitors and controls incoming and outgoing network traffic based on predetermined security rules.
- Back up your data: Regularly back up your important files to prevent data loss in the event of a cyber attack or other disaster.

By following these basic measures, you can significantly improve your cybersecurity posture and reduce your risk of falling victim to cyber threats.

CHAPTER THREE

Network Security

Network security refers to the practices and technologies used to secure networks and protect against cyber threats. This includes both physical and logical measures, such as firewalls, intrusion detection systems, and encryption.

Firewalls are a critical component of network security. They are software or hardware-based systems that monitor and control incoming and outgoing network traffic based on predetermined security rules. Firewalls can be configured to allow or block specific types of traffic, such as incoming connections from the internet or certain types of data.

Intrusion detection systems (IDS) are another important tool for network security. These systems monitor network traffic for signs of malicious activity, such as attempted attacks or unauthorized access. If an IDS detects suspicious activity, it can alert network administrators and take various actions to mitigate the threat.

Encryption is also an important aspect of network security. It involves the use of algorithms to encode data in such a way that it can only be accessed by someone with the correct decryption key. Encrypting sensitive data, such as passwords and financial information, can help to protect it from being accessed by unauthorized parties.

Overall, effective network security involves a combination of different measures and technologies, each of which plays a role in protecting against cyber threats.

CHAPTER FOUR

Cloud Security

Cloud security refers to the practices and technologies used to secure data and systems that are stored in the cloud. The cloud is a term used to describe a network of servers that are accessed over the internet, and it is becoming an increasingly popular way for individuals and organizations to store and access data.

One of the main benefits of the cloud is that it allows users to access their data from anywhere with an internet connection. However, this also means that protecting data in the cloud requires a different approach than traditional on-premises security.

Some of the key considerations for cloud security include:

- Data encryption: Encrypting data in the cloud can help to protect it from being accessed by unauthorized parties.
- Access controls: Establishing strong access controls and authentication methods can help to prevent unauthorized access to cloud-based systems and data.
- Security monitoring: Regularly monitoring cloud-based systems for signs of suspicious activity can help to detect and prevent cyber threats.
- Vendor security: It is important to carefully evaluate the security practices of cloud service providers and ensure that they meet your organization's standards.

By following best practices and implementing appropriate security measures, organizations can effectively protect their data and systems in the cloud.

CHAPTER FIVE

Mobile Security

Mobile security refers to the practices and technologies used to secure mobile devices, such as smartphones and tablets, and protect against mobile-specific threats.

- Mobile devices are vulnerable to a variety of threats, including malware, phishing attacks, and unauthorized access. In order to protect against these threats, it is important to take the following steps:
- Use a security app: Install a security app that can detect and remove malware, block unwanted calls and texts, and protect against phishing attacks.
- Keep your software up to date: Regularly update your operating system and other software to protect against security vulnerabilities.
- Use strong and unique passwords: Use a combination of letters, numbers, and special characters in your passwords, and avoid using the same password for multiple accounts.
- Enable two-factor authentication: Two-factor authentication (2FA) adds an extra layer of security by requiring you to provide a second form of verification, such as a code sent to your phone, in addition to your password.
- Be cautious when downloading apps: Only download apps from reputable sources, and be sure to read reviews and permissions before installing.

By following these steps, you can significantly improve the security of your mobile devices and protect against mobile-specific threats.

CHAPTER SIX

Cyber security Risk Management

Risk management is an important aspect of cybersecurity, and involves identifying, evaluating, and mitigating the risks associated with cyber threats.

There are several steps involved in effective risk management:

- Identify the risks: Identify the assets (such as data, systems, and devices) that are critical to your organization, and assess the potential risks to those assets. This may include internal threats, such as employee negligence or malicious intent, as well as external threats, such as hackers or cyber attacks.
- Evaluate the risks: Once the risks have been identified, they should be evaluated in terms of their likelihood and impact. This will help you to prioritize the risks and determine which ones require the most attention.
- Mitigate the risks: Develop and implement strategies for mitigating the identified risks. This may include implementing technical controls, such as firewalls and intrusion detection systems, or establishing policies and procedures for employees.
- Monitor and review: Regularly monitor the effectiveness of your risk mitigation strategies, and be prepared to adapt them as needed in response to changing threats or circumstances.

By following these steps, you can effectively manage the risks associated with cyber threats and improve your organization's overall cybersecurity posture.

CHAPTER SEVEN

Incident Response

Incident response refers to the process of responding to and recovering from a cyber attack or data breach. It is an essential part of any organization's cybersecurity strategy, and involves the following steps:

- Preparation: Develop and test an incident response plan, and ensure that all relevant personnel are trained on their roles and responsibilities.
- Detection: Monitor for signs of a cyber attack or data breach, and establish processes for quickly identifying and responding to incidents.
- Containment: Take immediate action to stop the attack and prevent it from spreading. This may include disconnecting affected systems from the network, activating incident response protocols, or involving law enforcement.
- Analysis: Investigate the incident to determine the extent of the damage and the nature of the attack.
- Recovery: Take steps to restore affected systems and data to their pre-incident state. This may include repairing or rebuilding systems, recovering data from backups, or implementing additional security measures.
- Post-incident review: After the incident has been resolved, conduct a review to identify any lessons learned and improve the incident response plan for future incidents.

By having a well-defined incident response plan in place and regularly testing and reviewing it, organizations can be better prepared to handle cyber attacks and minimize the impact of a data breach.

CHAPTER EIGHT

Compliance

Compliance refers to the process of ensuring that an organization's practices and policies align with relevant laws and regulations. In the field of cybersecurity, compliance is important in order to protect sensitive data and ensure that an organization is taking appropriate measures to secure its systems and networks.

There are several laws and regulations that relate to cybersecurity and the protection of sensitive data. These include:

- The General Data Protection Regulation (GDPR): A European Union (EU) law that regulates the collection and processing of personal data.
- The Health Insurance Portability and Accountability Act (HIPAA): A US law that regulates the handling of personal health information.
- The Payment Card Industry Data Security Standard (PCI DSS): A set of security standards that apply to organizations that process credit card transactions.
- The Sarbanes-Oxley Act (SOX): A US law that regulates the handling of financial information and requires organizations to implement internal controls and safeguards.

In order to ensure compliance with these and other laws and regulations, organizations should establish policies and procedures for protecting sensitive data, regularly monitor and review their cybersecurity practices, and provide training for employees on relevant compliance requirements. By doing so, organizations can protect against data breaches and other cyber threats and avoid the potential consequences of non-compliance.

CHAPTER NINE

Cybersecurity Trends and Best Practices

The field of cybersecurity is constantly evolving, and it is important for professionals to stay up-to-date on the latest trends and best practices in order to effectively protect against cyber threats. Some of the current trends and best practices in cybersecurity include:

- Artificial intelligence (AI) and machine learning: The use of AI and machine learning can help to improve the efficiency and effectiveness of cybersecurity measures, such as by detecting and responding to threats in real-time.
- The internet of things (IoT): The increasing proliferation of connected devices brings with it new security challenges, and it is important to implement appropriate security measures to protect against IoT-specific threats.
- Cloud security: As more organizations move to the cloud, it is important to carefully evaluate the security practices of cloud service providers and implement appropriate measures to secure cloud-based systems and data.
- Cybersecurity awareness training: Providing regular training for employees on cybersecurity best practices, such as strong password creation and the importance of updating software, can help to reduce the risk of cyber attacks.
- Multi-factor authentication: In addition to passwords, the use of additional authentication factors, such as biometric authentication or security tokens, can help to improve the security of systems and networks.

By staying up-to-date on these and other trends and best practices, organizations can improve their cybersecurity posture and protect against evolving cyber threats.

CHAPTER TEN

Professional Certification for Cyber security

Professional certification is an important way for cybersecurity professionals to demonstrate their expertise and commitment to the field. There are a number of certification programs available, each of which focuses on different aspects of cybersecurity and is geared towards different levels of experience.

Some popular certification programs for cybersecurity professionals include:

- Certified Information Systems Security Professional (CISSP): A vendor-neutral certification that covers a wide range of security topics and is suitable for experienced professionals.
- Certified Information Security Manager (CISM): A certification that focuses on the management of security programs and is aimed at professionals with at least five years of experience in the field.
- Certified Ethical Hacker (CEH): A certification that teaches professionals how to identify and exploit security vulnerabilities, and is suitable for those interested in penetration testing and ethical hacking.
- Certified Cloud Security Professional (CCSP): A certification that covers the specific security considerations associated with cloud computing and is suitable for professionals working in cloud security.
- Certified Information Systems Auditor (CISA): A certification that focuses on auditing and control of information systems, and is suitable for professionals with experience in this area.

By earning a professional certification, cybersecurity professionals can demonstrate their knowledge and skills to employers and advance their careers. It is important to carefully evaluate the different certification programs available and choose one that aligns with your career goals and level of experience.

CHAPTER ELEVEN

Scope of Cyber security in Future

The scope of cybersecurity is expected to continue to grow and evolve in the future as technology advances and the reliance on digital systems increases. Some of the key trends and developments that are likely to shape the future of cybersecurity include:

- The increasing use of artificial intelligence (AI) and machine learning: AI and machine learning are expected to play a larger role in cybersecurity in the future, with the potential to improve the efficiency and effectiveness of security measures.
- The proliferation of the internet of things (IoT): The increasing number of connected devices is expected to bring with it new security challenges, and cybersecurity professionals will need to be equipped to handle these challenges.
- The increasing adoption of cloud computing: As more organizations move to the cloud, there will be a need for professionals with expertise in cloud security.
- Cybersecurity regulation: As the importance of cybersecurity continues to be recognized, it is likely that there will be an increase in the number and scope of laws and regulations related to cybersecurity.
- Cybersecurity as a critical infrastructure: As our reliance on digital systems increases, cybersecurity is expected to become even more critical to the functioning of society, including critical infrastructure such as power plants and transportation systems.

Overall, the future of cybersecurity is likely to involve a continued focus on the protection of digital systems, networks, and devices from cyber threats. It is an important and rapidly-evolving field that will continue to be in high demand.

CHAPTER TWELVE

Advantages of Cyber security

There are numerous advantages to implementing effective cybersecurity measures, including:

1. Protection of sensitive data: Cybersecurity helps to protect sensitive data, such as financial information and personal identification, from being accessed or compromised by unauthorized parties.
2. Prevention of data breaches: By implementing appropriate security measures, organizations can prevent data breaches and the potential consequences, such as financial losses and damage to reputation.
3. Compliance with laws and regulations: Cybersecurity can help organizations to comply with laws and regulations related to the protection of sensitive data, such as the General Data Protection Regulation (GDPR) and the Health Insurance Portability and Accountability Act (HIPAA).
4. Enhanced customer trust: By demonstrating a commitment to cybersecurity, organizations can build trust with customers and improve their perception of the organization.
5. Improved operational efficiency: Effective cybersecurity can help to prevent disruptions caused by cyber attacks, allowing organizations to operate more efficiently.

Overall, implementing strong cybersecurity measures can help organizations to protect against cyber threats and realize a range of benefits.

CHAPTER THIRTEEN

Cyber security interview questions

Differentiate between threat, vulnerability and risk

In the context of cybersecurity, a threat refers to a potential source of harm or danger, such as a hacker or a virus. A vulnerability is a weakness or gap in an organization's defenses that could be exploited by a threat. Risk is the potential impact or consequence of a threat exploiting a vulnerability.

For example, a hacker attempting to gain access to an organization's systems would be a threat. If the organization's systems are not adequately protected with strong passwords and firewalls, they may have a vulnerability that the hacker could exploit. The risk in this case would be the potential damage or consequences of the hacker successfully accessing the systems, such as the theft of sensitive data or disruption of operations.

In order to effectively protect against cyber threats, it is important to identify and evaluate both the threats and vulnerabilities that an organization faces, and to implement measures to mitigate the resulting risks.

Who are Black Hat, White Hat and Grey Hat Hackers?

Black hat hackers are individuals who use their skills to gain unauthorized access to systems or to steal sensitive information. They are often motivated by financial gain, personal mischief, or a desire to cause harm. Black hat hacking is illegal and can result in severe consequences.

White hat hackers, on the other hand, are ethical hackers who use their skills to help organizations identify and fix vulnerabilities in their systems.

White hat hacking is legal and is often done with the permission of the organizations being tested.

Grey hat hackers are a mixture of both black hat and white hat hackers. They may use their skills to gain unauthorized access to systems, but they do so with the intention of alerting the organizations to the vulnerabilities that they have discovered and helping them to fix them. Grey hat hacking is a controversial area, as it involves activities that are technically illegal, but may be done with the best of intentions.

What are the types of Cyber Security?

There are several types of cybersecurity that are designed to protect against different types of threats and vulnerabilities. Some common types of cybersecurity include:

- Network security: This type of cybersecurity focuses on protecting the integrity and confidentiality of data as it is transmitted over networks. It includes measures such as firewalls, intrusion detection systems, and encryption.
- Endpoint security: This type of cybersecurity is concerned with protecting individual devices, such as computers, smartphones, and tablets, from threats. It includes measures such as antivirus software and device firewall.
- Application security: This type of cybersecurity focuses on protecting the security of software applications and systems. It includes measures such as input validation and secure coding practices.
- Cloud security: This type of cybersecurity is concerned with protecting data and systems that are stored in the cloud. It includes measures such as encryption and access controls.
- Internet of things (IoT) security: This type of cybersecurity is focused on protecting connected devices, such as smart home devices, from threats. It includes measures such as secure software updates and strong passwords.

Overall, effective cybersecurity involves a combination of different types of measures, each of which is designed to protect against specific types of threats and vulnerabilities.

Define Cryptography.

Cryptography is the practice of secure communication in the presence of third parties. It involves the use of mathematical algorithms and protocols to encode and decode messages, ensuring that only authorized parties can access the information being transmitted. Cryptography is used in a variety of contexts, including to protect sensitive data during online transactions, to secure communications between military or government agencies, and to ensure the confidentiality of personal or proprietary information.

Differentiate between IDS and IPS.

Intrusion Detection System (IDS) and Intrusion Prevention System (IPS) are both security technologies that are used to protect computer networks from external threats.

An IDS is a system that is designed to detect security threats and anomalies within a network. It analyzes network traffic and system logs to identify signs of an attack or unauthorized access. When an IDS detects an issue, it will alert the network administrator so that they can take appropriate action. However, it does not take any active steps to prevent the attack from occurring.

An IPS, on the other hand, is a system that is designed to actively prevent security threats and anomalies. It analyzes network traffic in real-time and takes action to block or mitigate any detected threats. An IPS can be configured to take a variety of actions, such as blocking specific traffic, quarantining suspicious packets, or even shutting down a network connection if necessary.

What is CIA?

CIA is an acronym that stands for Confidentiality, Integrity, and Availability. These three principles are the cornerstone of information security.

- Confidentiality refers to the protection of information from unauthorized access or disclosure. It is concerned with ensuring that sensitive information is only accessible to those who are authorized to see it.

- Integrity refers to the protection of information from unauthorized modification or tampering. It is concerned with ensuring that the information is accurate, complete, and uncorrupted.
- Availability refers to the ability of authorized users to access information when they need it. It is concerned with ensuring that the systems and resources required to access the information are functioning properly and are available to those who need them.

Together, these three principles form the foundation of a secure information system. Ensuring the CIA of information is essential to protecting the confidentiality, integrity, and availability of data and systems.

What is a Firewall?

A firewall is a security system that controls incoming and outgoing network traffic based on predetermined security rules. A firewall can be hardware-based, software-based, or a combination of both.

The primary function of a firewall is to block unwanted traffic and to allow authorized traffic. It does this by examining the data packets that are transmitted over a network and determining whether they should be allowed through based on the security rules that have been configured. A firewall can be configured to allow or block traffic based on various criteria, such as the source or destination of the traffic, the type of traffic, or the port number that is being used.

Firewalls are often used to protect a network from external threats, such as hackers and malware. They can also be used to enforce security policies and to monitor network activity for suspicious behavior. Firewalls are an essential component of a secure network and are often used in conjunction with other security technologies, such as antivirus software and intrusion prevention systems.

Glossary

1. Antivirus software: Software that is designed to detect and remove computer viruses and other malicious software.
2. Firewall: A security system that controls incoming and outgoing network traffic based on predetermined security rules.
3. Malware: Short for "malicious software," malware is any software that is designed to harm or exploit computer systems.
4. Phishing: A type of cyber attack that involves attempting to trick individuals into revealing sensitive information, such as passwords or financial data, by posing as a legitimate entity.
5. Two-factor authentication: A security process that requires an additional piece of information, such as a code sent to a phone, in addition to a username and password in order to log in.
6. Virus: A piece of code that is designed to replicate itself and spread from one computer to another, often with malicious intent.
7. Vulnerability: A weakness or flaw in a computer system or piece of software that could be exploited by an attacker.
8. Whitelist: A list of approved or trusted sources, such as websites or email addresses, that are allowed to access a system or network.
9. Blacklist: A list of sources, such as websites or email addresses, that are not allowed to access a system or network.